Line and Letter Tracing: Alphabet and Sight Words

ISBN: 9798686106246

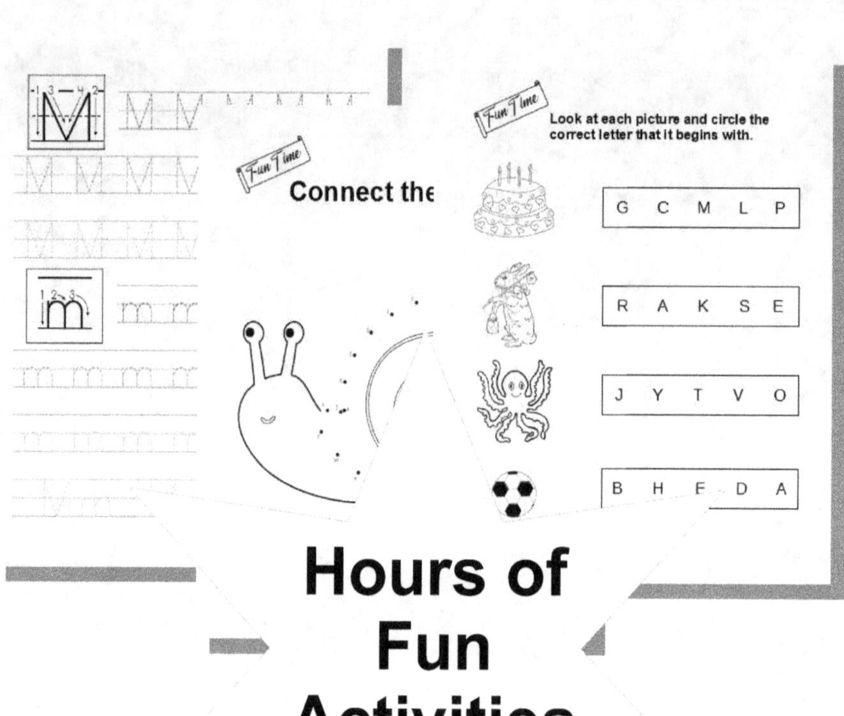

Hours of
Fun
Activities

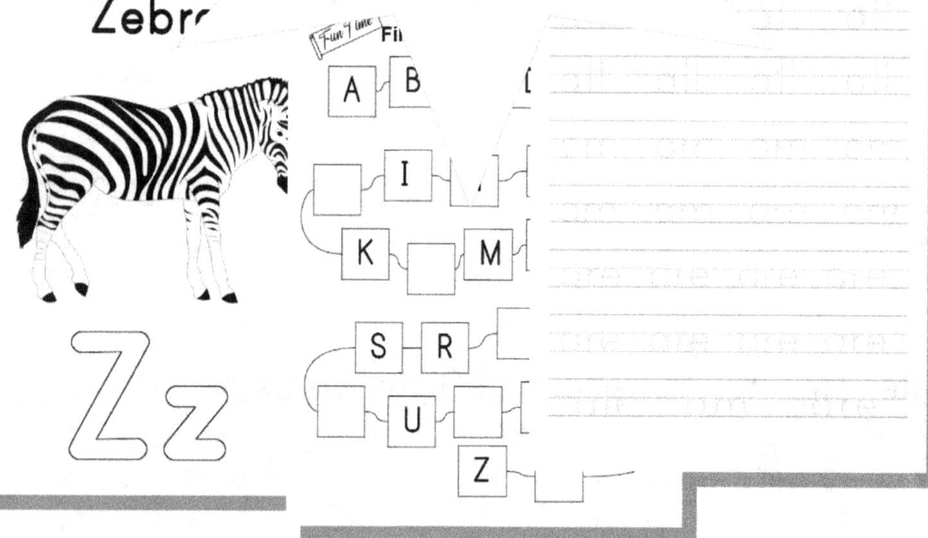

This book belongs
to

____

____

Trace the lines

Shapes

Square

Triangle

Circle

House

Bee

Key

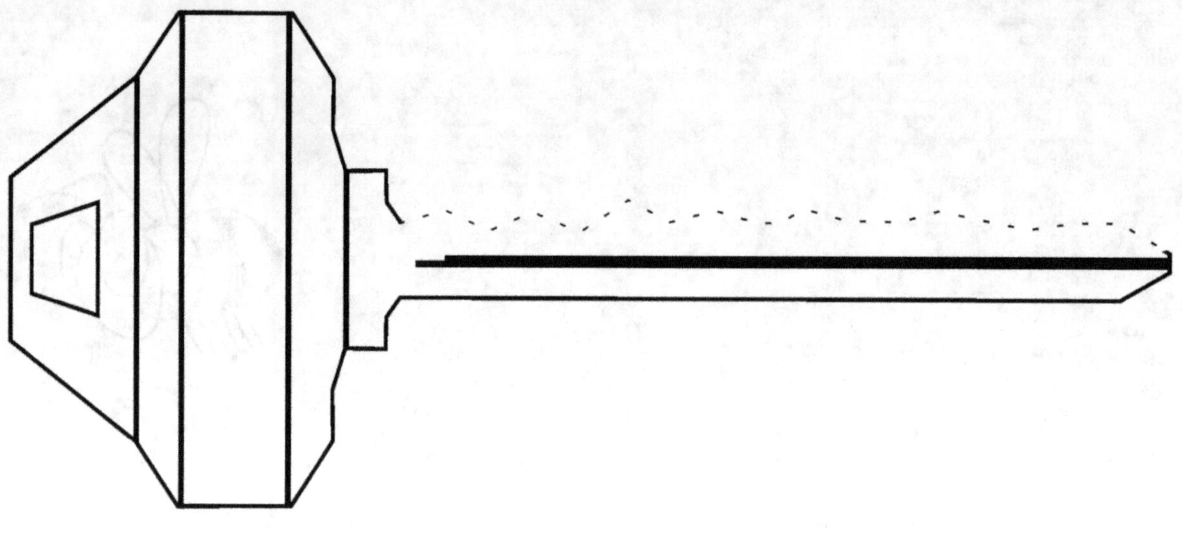

Alphabet
Trace the letters

Apple

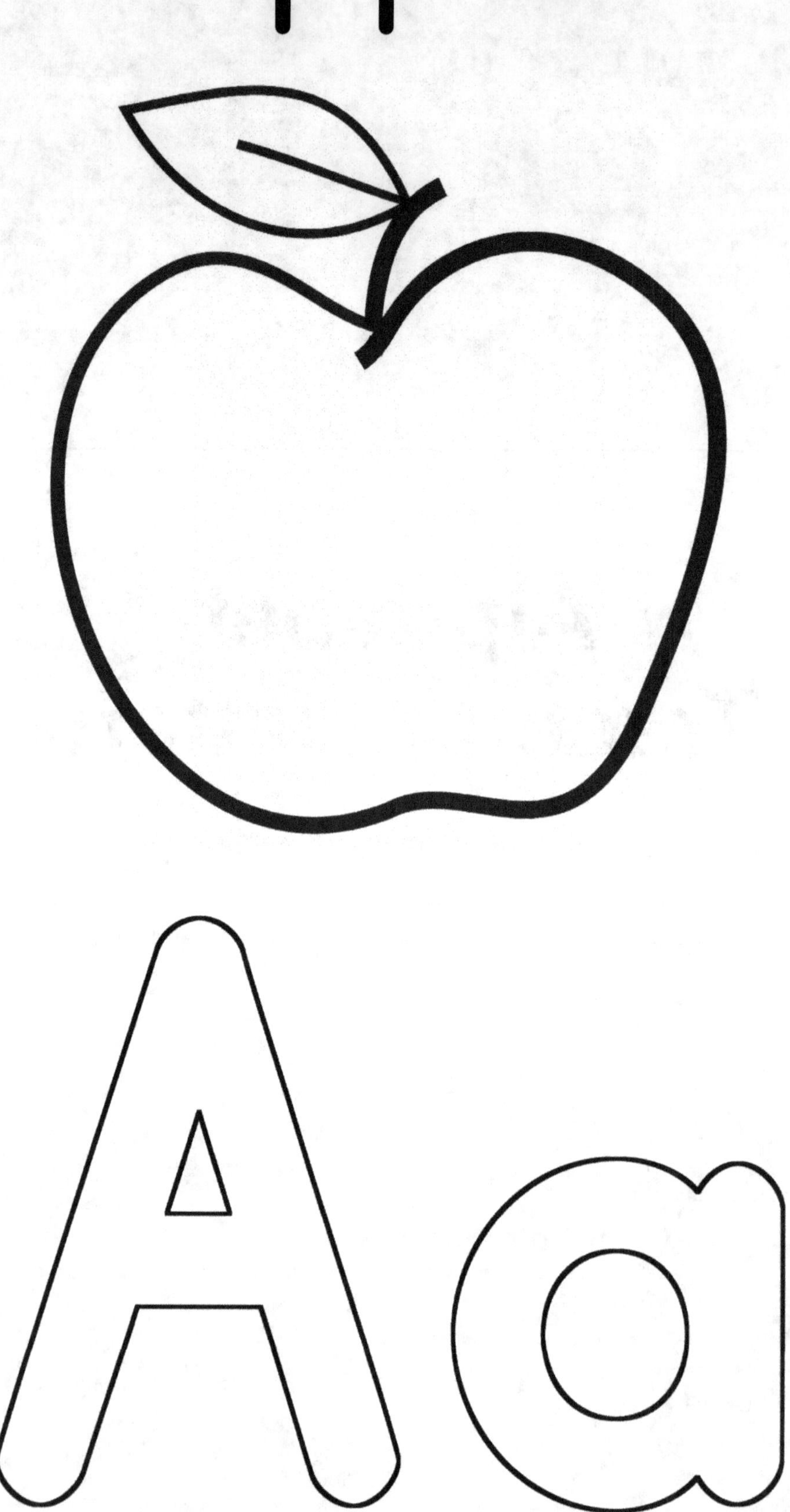

Bird

Bb

Car

Cc

Dog

Dd

Elephant

E e

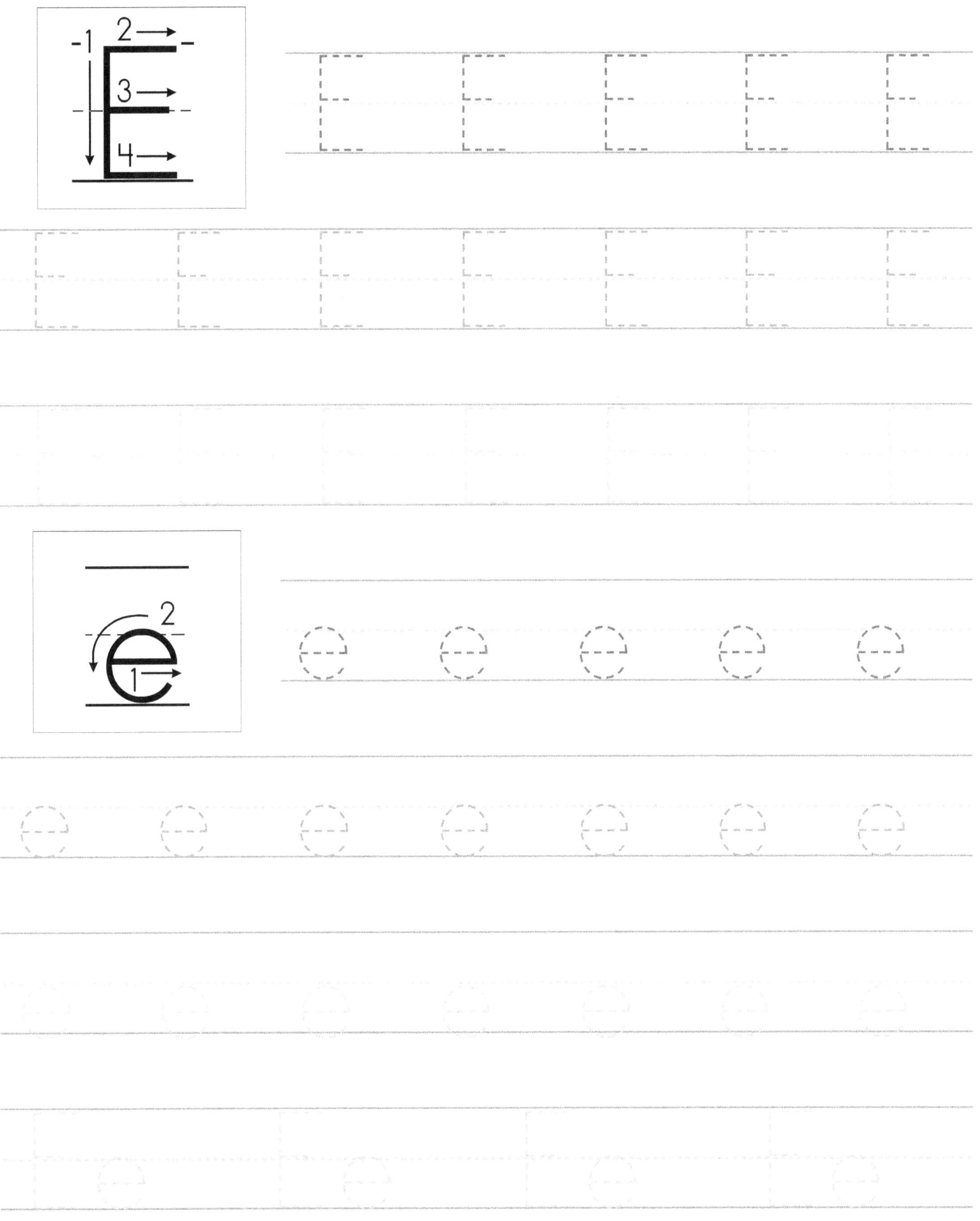

Fish

F f

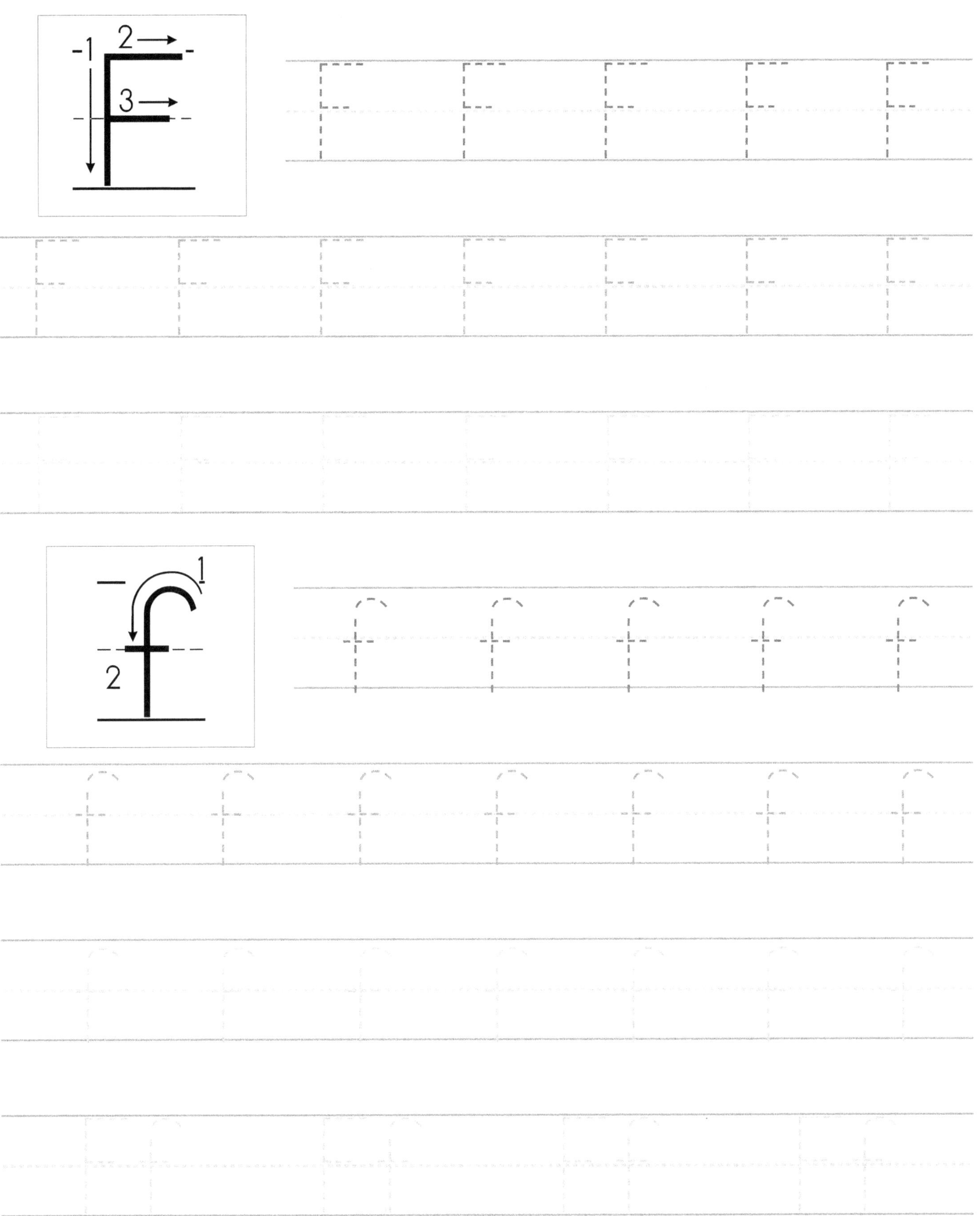

Goat

G g

Horse

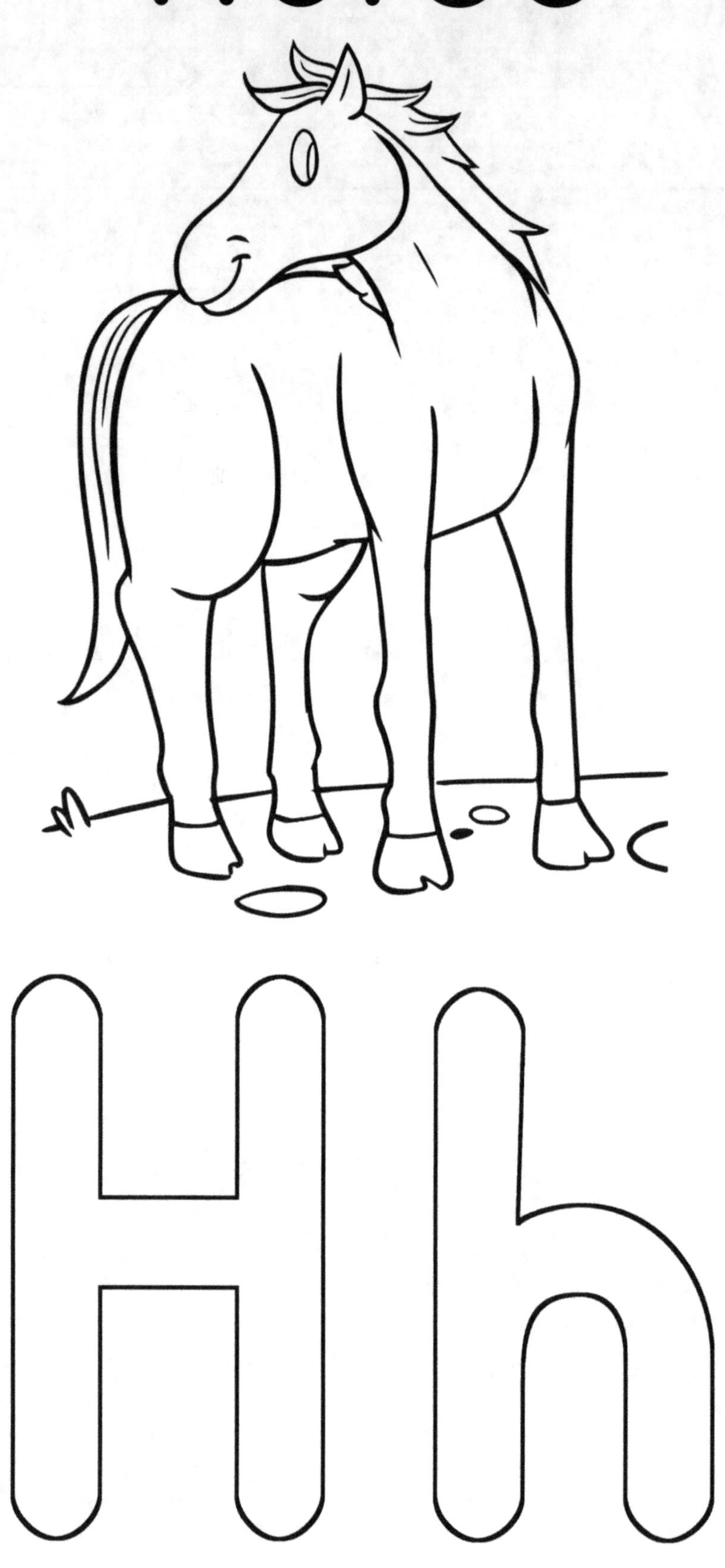

Hh

Ice cream

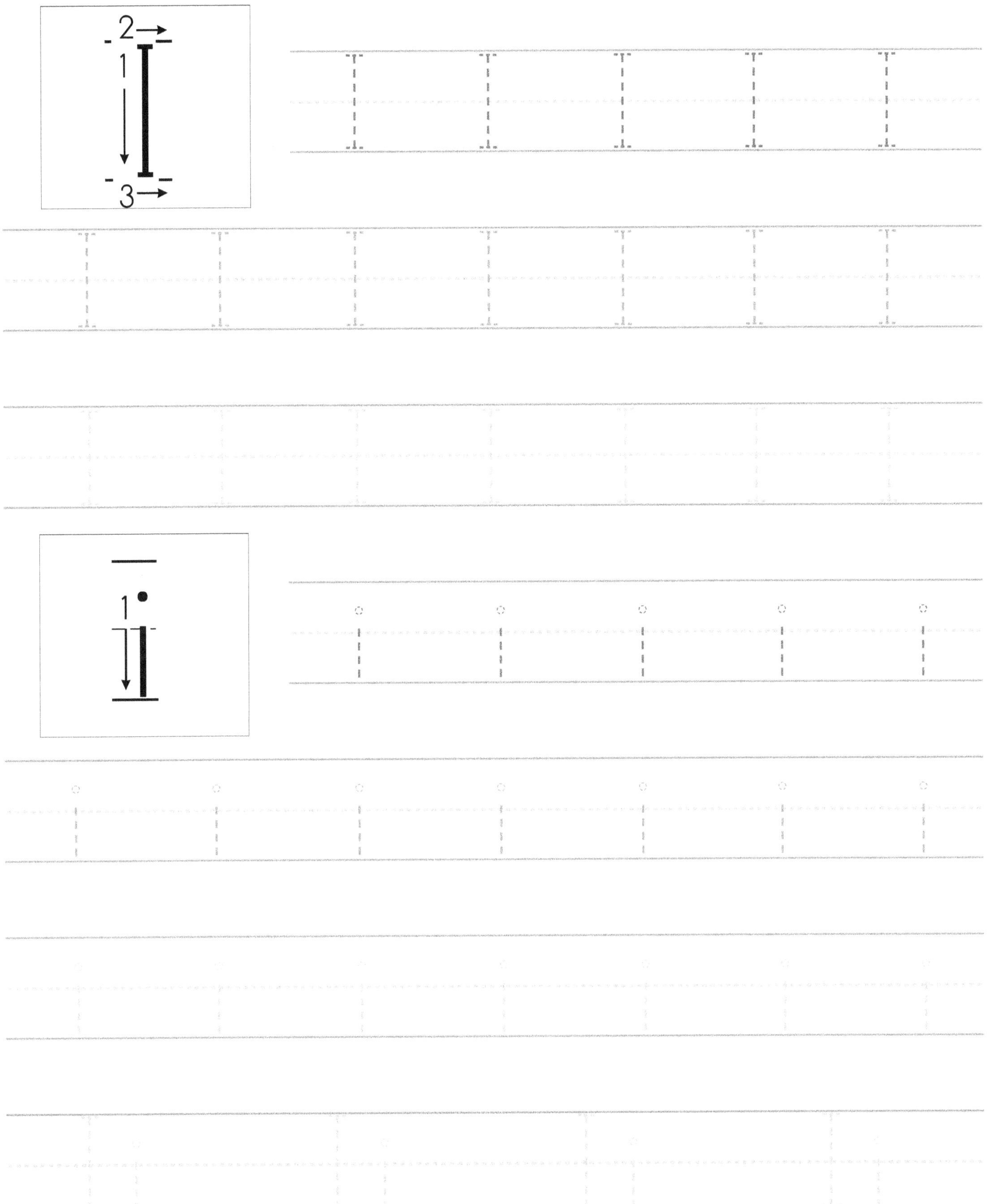

Connect the dots.

Look at each picture and circle the correct letter that it begins with.

G   C   M   L   P

R   A   K   S   E

J   Y   T   V   O

B   H   E   D   A

Jellyfish

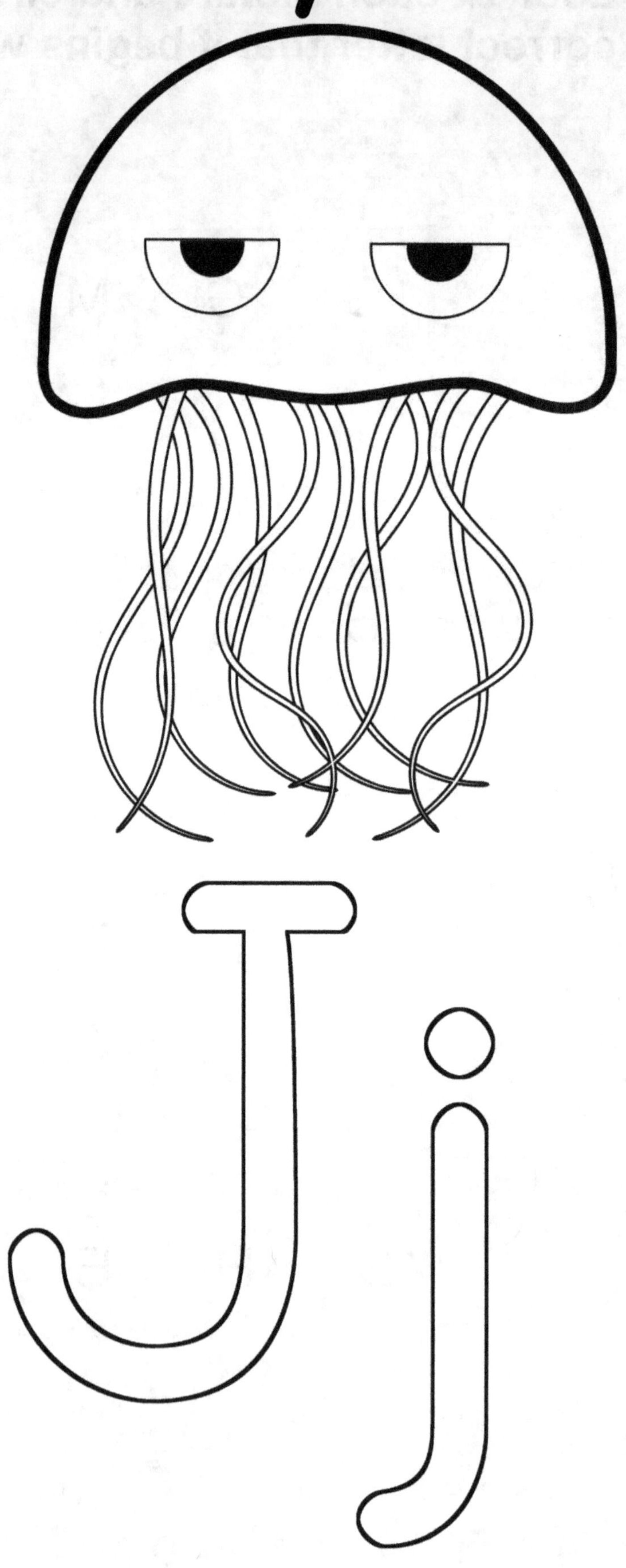

Kangaroo

K k

Lion

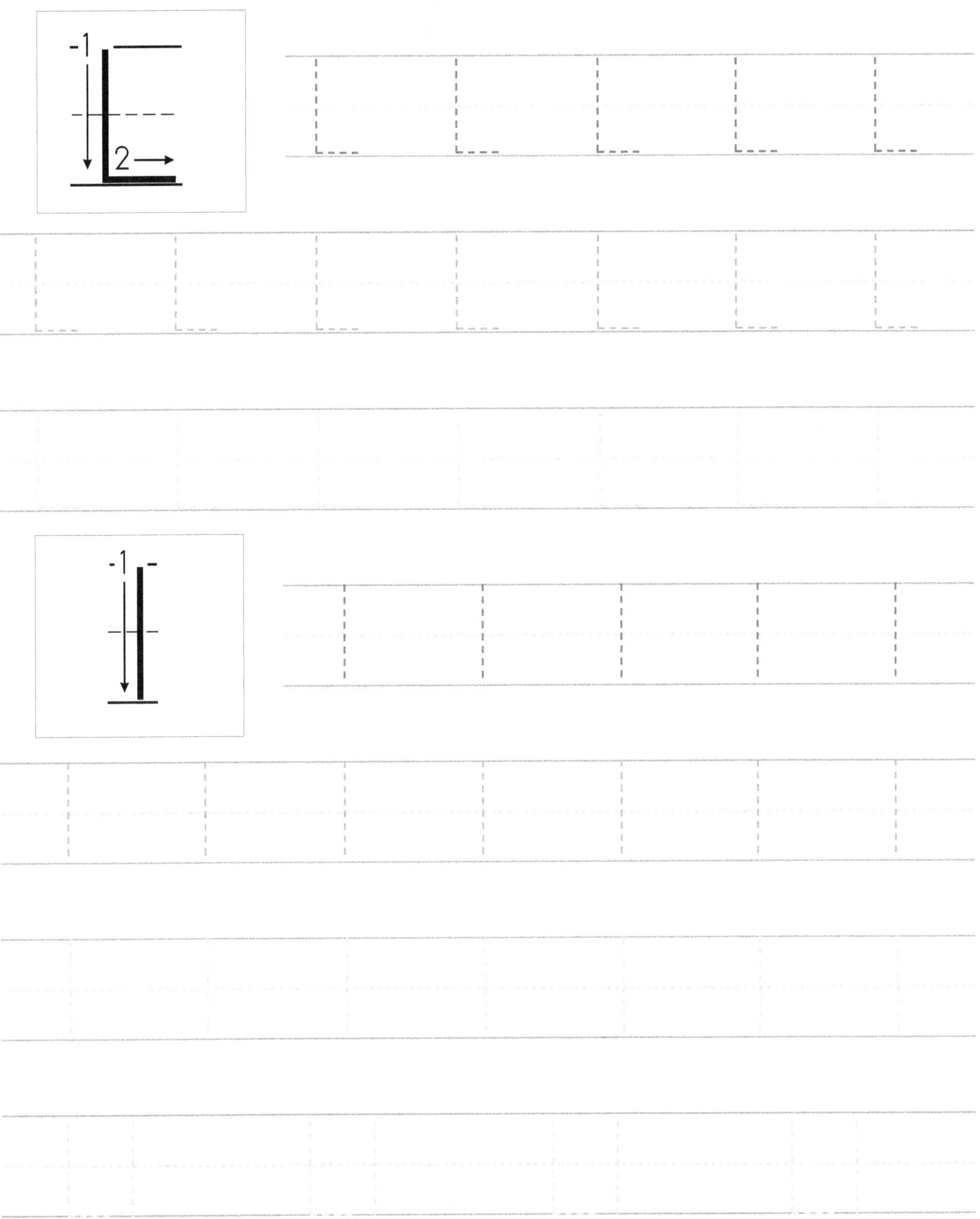

Monkey

M m

Net

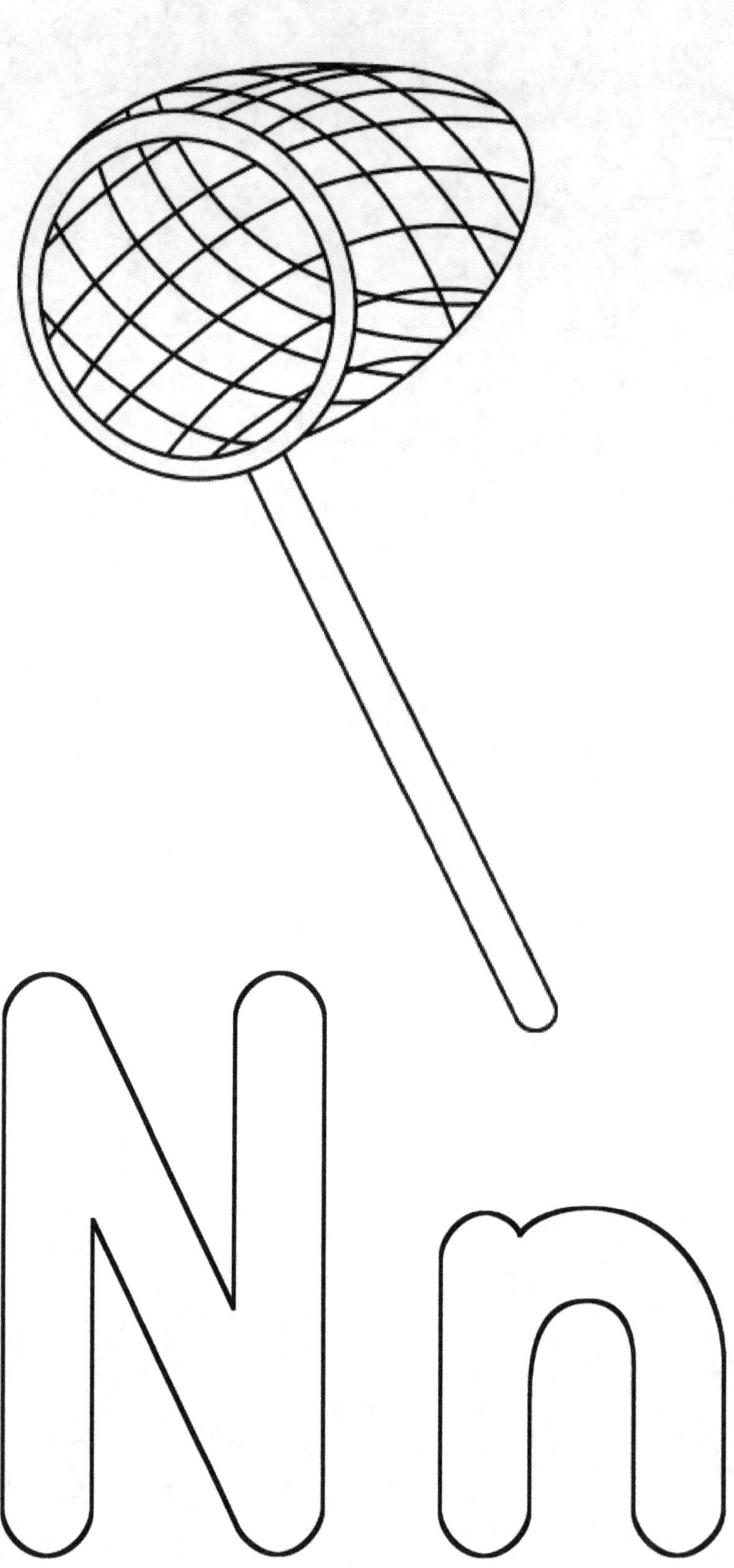

N n

Owl

Pig

P p

Queen

Q q

Rabbit

Connect the dots.

Look at each picture and circle the correct letter that it begins with.

D   A   S   J   Q

O   E   P   V   F

C   B   D   R   K

K   L   R   S   G

Squirrel

S s

Tiger

T t

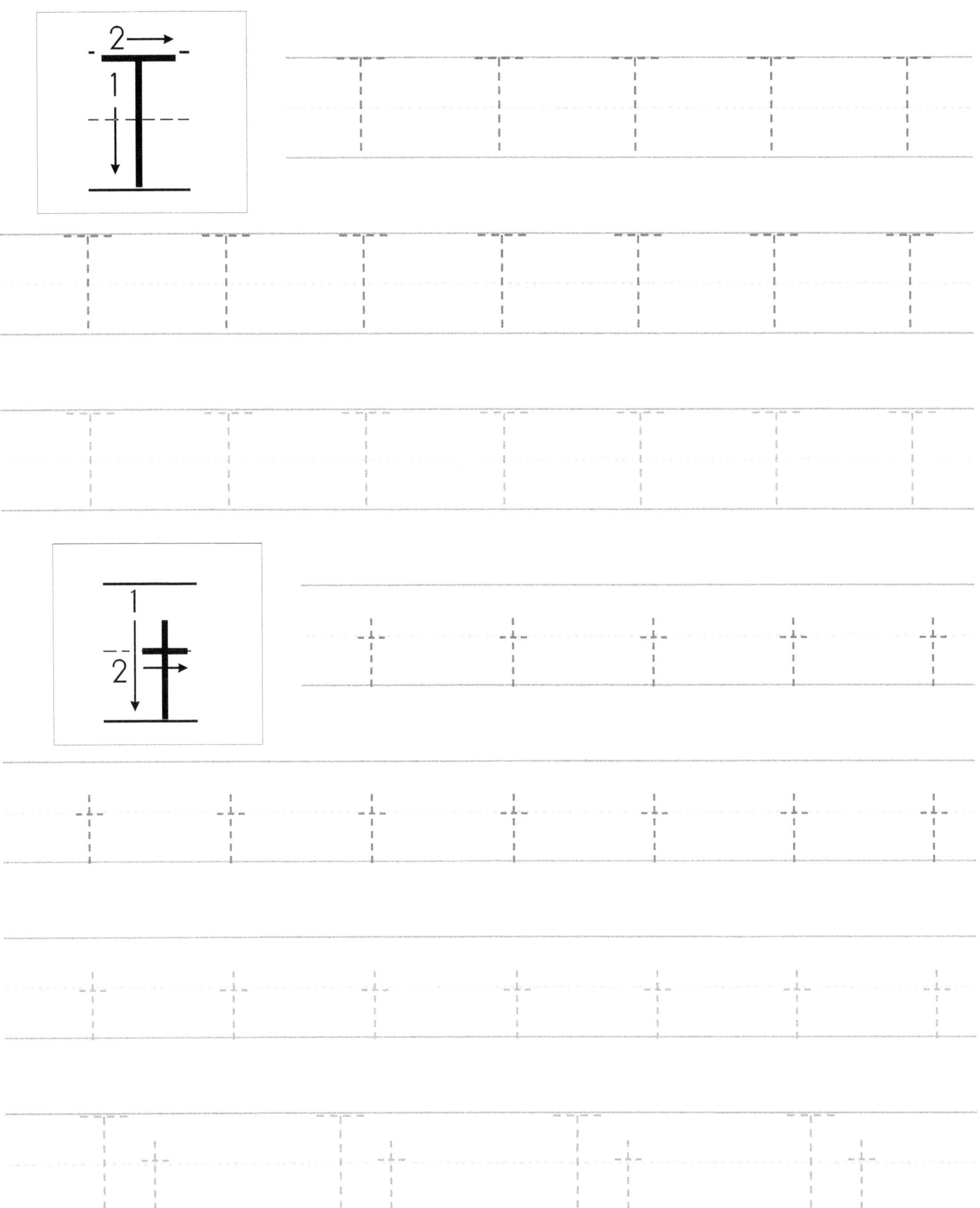

Unicorn

Uu

Vulture

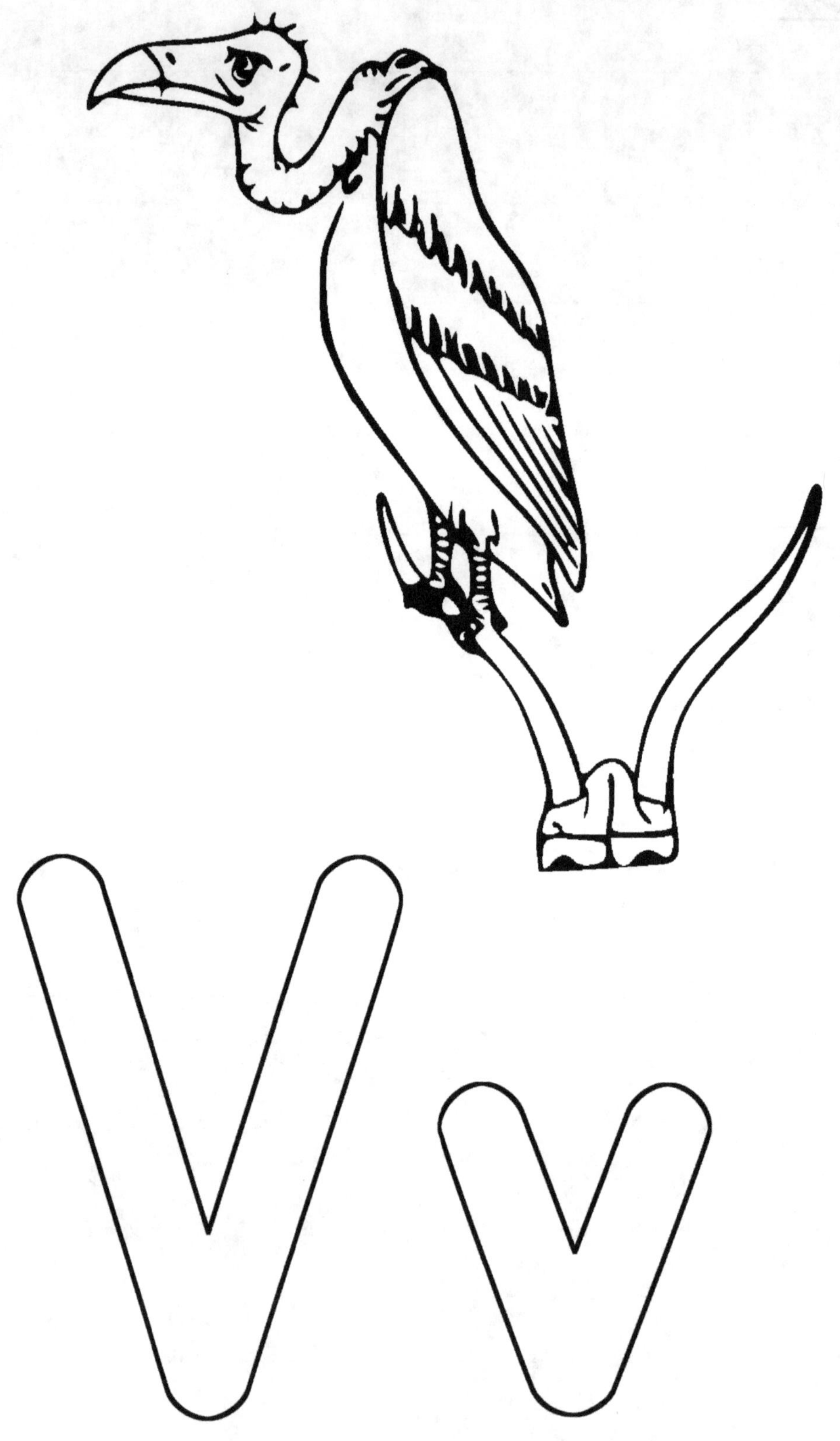

Whale

W w

Xylophone

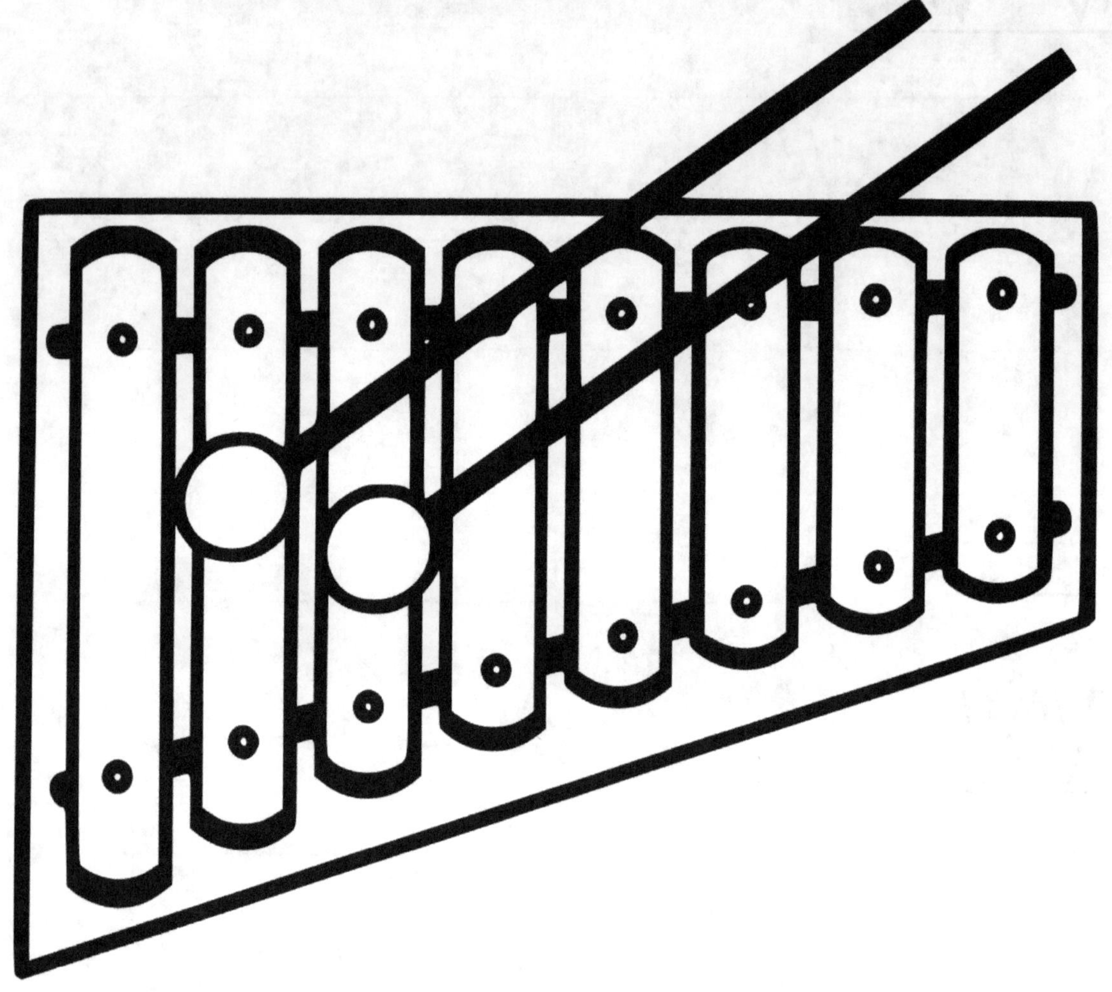

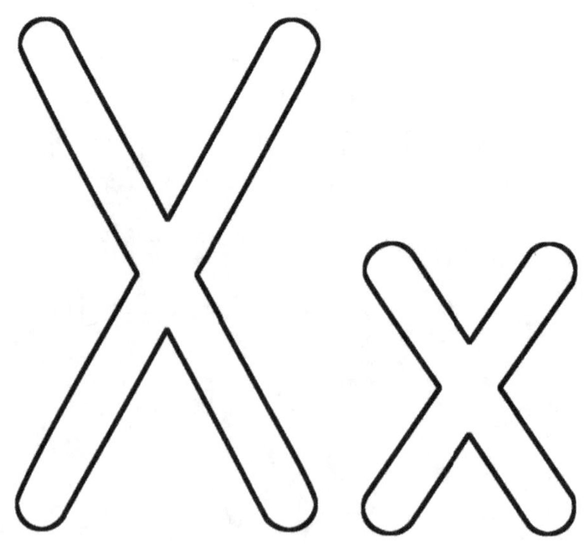

Yacht

Y y

Zebra

Zz

a b c d e
f g h i j
k l m n o
p q r s t
u v w x
y z

Fill in the missing alphabet.

Sight Words

all all all all

all all all all

am am am am

am am am am

are are are are

are are are are

all am are

at at at at at

at at at at

and and and

and and and

be be be be

be be be be

be be be be

but but but but

but but but but

can can can can

can can can can

come come come

come come come

but can come

down down down
down down down

eat eat eat eat

eat eat eat eat

find find find find

find find find

for for for for

for for for for

eat find for

get get get get
get get get get
has has has has
has has has has
have have have
have have have
get has have

into into into into

into into into

like like like like

like like like like

into like like

must must must

must must must

make make make

make make make

now now now

now now now

must make now

new new new
new new new
out out out out
out out out out
out out out out
out out out out
new out out

play play play play

play play play play

run run run run

run run run run

see see see see

see see see see

play run see

she she she she
she she she she
said said said
said said said
that that that
that that that
she said that

this this this
this this this
there there there
there there there
too too too too
too too too too
this there too

they they they

they they they

want want want

want want want

want want want

want want want

they want want

when when when

when when when

where   where

where   where

which   which

which   which

when where which

walk   walk   walk

walk   walk   walk

yes   yes   yes   yes

yes   yes   yes   yes

you   you   you   you

you   you   you   you

walk   yes   you

More Practice

Form your own words or sentences
and keep practicing.

Answers

 G (C) M L P

 (R) A K S E

 J Y T V (O)

 (B) H E D A

 (D) A S J Q

 O E (P) V F

 C B D R (K)

 K L (R) S G